FRANCESCO PRIMERANO

Google, Twitter, Facebook & Youtube:

1000 Dreams, Music Stars & Love Stories

The Best of Pink Floyd Queen Beatles Rolling Stones
J.Lennon F.Mercury M.Monroe Mina. V.Rossi R. Zero

Youcanprint *Self-Publishing*

Are Life, Poetry, the Music, Cinema and love in all their splendor

The great values and symbols that have left an important mark on our lives

Our favorite social networks (Google+, Twitter, Facebook and YouTube)

The notes and pages of Google, Twitter, Facebook & Youtube colors more 'variety, shapes and content more inviting, open, you browse, read, scrutinize, they love and then close with the hope and the desire to read them again with the same passion that was presented initially

(F.Primerano)

Titolo | Google, Twitter, Facebook & Youtube

Autore | Francesco Primerano

ISBN | 978-88-93061-51-3

Youcanprint Self-Publishing

Via Roma, 73 – 73039 Tricase (LE) – Italy

www.youcanprint.it

info@youcanprint.it

Facebook: facebook.com/youcanprint.it

Twitter: twitter.com/youcanprintit

TABLE OF CONTENTS

INTRODUCTION

From our pure essence you can be perceived traces of a healthy ego and innocent that it would never end in obvious and intrusive events of conceit and arrogance, but not in the corny and fake attitudes of humility. Besides, in this world of false and hypocritical, signed also by the presence of Google, Twitter, Facebook and YouTube, it could not be anything other than the delusional exhibitionists and sympathetic villains. But this obvious and simple story is our soul winning, nothing but her. The emotions that we live, the thoughts and the words we speak and write daily in the large garden of our lives are nothing but precious pearls that we guard jealously and at the same time show off with grace and delight, are nothing more than poetic notes, music, art that we love petting and live to the full, but those same emotions that we try to live in full may be simply delicious cherries we enjoy with pleasure, one after another, also between the notes, dreams, myths and colors of the three social networks more popular in this period. "4 Names, 4 legends" could define them exactly. Yet we have tasted in many and we continue to explore them willingly. You may wonder what ever is talking about !? Obviously phenomena Google, Twitter, Facebook & Youtube, which are affecting millions of people around the world. 4 Events truly special and brilliant where you meet different personalities, all the colors of humanity, values and cowardice of our existence, the worst delights and also the best indecencies. The manual in question you want to present simply as an attractive collection of nectar of life, poetic and innocent thoughts and inviting aphorisms that make us to better understand not only the reality of Google, Twitter, Facebook & Youtube in their multiple aspects but also the everyday life. Essentially they describe with great fervor and interest notes poetic, musical, emotional, artistic representing

in full the era of Google, Twitter, Facebook &
Youtube. Notes strictly written and described in
great detail by the author and accompanied by
intriguing aspects and images that have signed
the world of art in its best expression, by the
magic of the goddess Poetry Music, by the
Cinema Theatre, from Pink Floyd to Queen, Mina
at Barbra Streisand, from the Beatles to the
Rolling Stones, from Vasco Rossi to Renato Zero,
from Marilyn Monroe to Brigitte Bardot, by John
Lennon, Freddie Mercury, Totò, Roberto Benigni,
from Pablo Neruda to Paolo Coelho, its
landscapes the wonders of Rome, the magical
song of the dolphins to the songs of Rock Music,
from artists of great depth to those of less
significance.

FIRST CHAPTER

Social networks live with in us

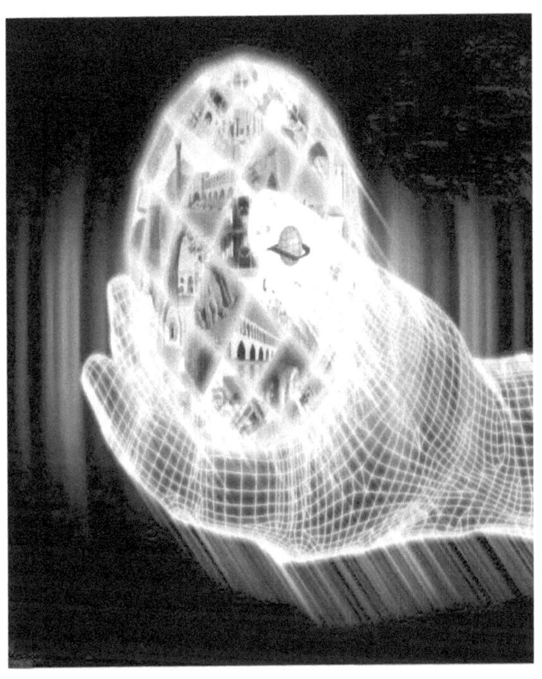

It is now very late to go back in steps and in the various journeys healthy, practical and tangible that we had chosen to go. All of us we feed Google, Twitter, Facebook & Youtube, as the flies eat the best crap, but we like these things, we have always attracted and fascinated. These infernal machines will appear very attractive and pleasant, all of humanity can not do without it because it would not be able to do nothing but destroy everything that is healthy and practical, at least what little there was left. You may define evil machines designed to corrupt our reason and to deprive us of our common sense !? Curiosity got the best of us and the mental chaos meant that we us to contact them !? They promised order and peace in return for our obedient and silent consent !? No, none of that. Social networks present themselves simply as special events and genial, where you meet different personalities, all the colors of humanity, values and cowardice of our existence, the worst delights and also the best indecencies. "4 names, 4 legends", we could be defined exactly.

♪ ♫ It 's always interesting to surf the Internet, but the most intriguing surf the wonderful ocean of adventure and fun. ♪

Yet Google, Twitter, Facebook & Youtube have

entered our daily lives, in our guts, in our homes, in our minds, in our offices, in our dreams, in our cars, in our gestures, in our pockets, in our speeches, in our thoughts, and we we welcomed them with good humor and wonder, with great passion and at the same time with a little choked up. Now part of us, silent within us, but they live and whether they live are of us, if we are dying, and they talk about us, and this grows curious habit to Google, Twitter, Facebook & Youtube that basically we want alive. And they live with us, live, and open up within us, then continue to live, and expect the best time to grow again, end up with our day, and started again when we can not send them away, they can not die, you make them die and live. Google, Twitter, Facebook & Youtube are always live within us with their notes and pages best, because it is impossible to do without. It 'was a big mistake he snubbed for so many years the world web. Currently you are aware more than ever that he had discovered a house definitely fantastic and welcoming, where you can create, build, people really know interesting that it allows you to feed their views and where to live a virtual life that is completely harmless and simply intriguing. It 'true that for several years he had ignored the web world has served to break out indoors and tedious considering great damage to expensive health and a kind of deprivation of liberty, preferring always to the exits that open navigations in virtual worlds completely unnecessary, but it is equally true that it was considered a real renunciation of something founded and concrete that is part of our great culture. A few years later he manages to evaluate with great fervor Mr. Internet appreciating its potential definitely positive and allowed us to take advantage of the creativity and the desire to build. Basically we did find some very special people and allowed us to realize interesting collaborations, activities that we never imagined to undertake, real passions turned into rewarding activities especially in terms of moral and professional. We should thank the often temporary world for his willingness to make himself known, discover, explore, sniff, scrutinize. This and more is the Web with its nuances and its variegated colors, smells and tastes. From all this we can deduce that in life it 's never too late to discover the reality that you wast quite distant from you, and for these and other essential reasons it would be advisable to dare and to continue to explore more and more of the pearls and treasures in the past they could be considered frivolous and without any sense. The same things you could easily do for phenomena Google, Twitter, Facebook & Youtube that affected millions of people around the world. The year was 2004, when an American kid Cambridge Mark Zuckerberg had the brilliant idea, along with his classmates, to found what would soon become the largest social network of all time. E 'managed to twist and change in a very positive the multiple aspects related to communication, socialization and interaction between individuals around the world, the human, emotional, economic, private, commercial, cultural, social and ethical. The world's largest social service currently has more than one billion subscribers. Users can set up and join groups to share common interests with others, organized by country of origin, the adopted city, workplace, university, school, or other characteristics, sharing of various content general media and use various applications on the site. Another company is very attractive Youtube, which, with a billion per month of contacts, seems to exceed in recent times the same Facebook in terms of users. Youtube is presented as just another platform, where they are permitted views and shares videos of any kind. Finally, the other company of great interest is Twitter, a platform created in March 2006 by Obvibus Corporation of San Francisco, where you can share thoughts and words of a maximum length of 140 characters. Google needs no introduction: it is the most effective search engine and world's most popular web. Essentially users turn out to be the moral and material wealth of these social services very attractive; actually they would not exist without them these infernal machines that have changed the habits of our dull existence. Sometimes we'd love to shout loudly: "How nice it would be if all we became a very good family, even though dispersed and rooted for the various areas of the world. A fantastic family who joins in good times and bad, in victory and in defeat, in joy and in pain. A nice group solid and supportive, a great carousel of adventures and experiences intensively by special people like us, we who belong to the fabulous era of Google, Twitter, Facebook & Youtube "

SECOND CHAPTER

1000 emotions of

Google, Twitter, Facebook & Youtube

Social are definitely present in different types of users affected by the contagion of pleasant Google, Twitter, Facebook & Youtube. It meets just about anything: look out divergent ideas, but also opinions shared by many or all. There is the housewife who thinks to find his favorite recipes, there's the student who finds himself immersed in a few pages of sports or music after a busy day of study, there is the group of young people who after a night from rocking disco will send messages only to say a simple and cursed "Hello", there is the worker who, after a day of hell, trying to find entertainment more just to recover. There are those who opens the door to happiness and those close to the truth, there is the cunning duty and idiot talented, there is a false feel-good and the asshole, there are those who judge without knowing to be a failed, the child is smiling and the adult who is desperate, there is rich in humility and honesty of the poor, there are those who give lessons in math without knowing how much is 2+2, and who gives lessons life without knowing of being an idiot, is the librarian who fails and who denounces him for some rude, some lost in love and who wins in the game of life, there is the old lady who is husband and who becomes a father without knowing it, somebody turns off the pages and groups without warning, there is a young grandmother who gives the numbers preferring the mouse to his grandson, there's always that author that seeks to impose itself in publishing world and there Francis greets everyone wishing luck in this precious existence. The emotions that we live, the thoughts and the words we speak and write daily in the large garden of our lives are nothing but precious pearls that we guard jealously and at the same time show off with grace and delight, are nothing more than human notes, poetry and music, we love to caress and live to the full, but those same emotions that we try to live in full may be simply delicious cherries we enjoy with pleasure, one after another, even among the myths, dreams and colors Google, Twitter, Facebook & Youtube. There are those who, in the pages of social networks, can find himself consider ourselves even more, but it is only a true illusion or the attainment of a desired pleasure always !? There is also the kind that questions everything, even the pants wearing, and goes some way to bridge those gaps where you fell, expressing something like "an empty stomach I find myself immersed in a vacuum, in void of an empty room, in the vacuum of a love emptied by vacuum, the void of nothingness, I could not be that full of huge voids that were not able to be filled if not with my great soul who was not empty, but this huge void you can find the fullness of my existence by filling those tiny voids in the best way? "Between the pages of Social you can meet even those people who try in every way to satisfy those emotions that had died during a hellish day or in a matter of hours spent in nothing. In our lifetime we will carry out certain projects to meet their own emotions; these sometimes bend, but if you believe in it not ever be broken. Emotions will always be present if we live them intensely without worrying how to explain or understand them. There are those who admit to having always scrutinized and praised the positive and all the pleasant qualities of the human being, otherwise he would continue to hate the whole of humanity. Even if the animal is to be much higher you should always appreciate the people for those who are in their positivity and does not denigrating for what are not. Some people estimate as much for everything 'that has earned to the point of not caring about what you could present negative in the life of every moment for those who have the conscience clean and healthy as he has nothing to fear, and for this intriguing and exciting reason he continues to love yourself. Everybody this and very much hopes to be at the center of the world, but can not figure out what the Universe is at the center of our thoughts. Nothing is as before, but everything may look better than then. We need surprise us to fill a void, but the surprise will never be enough to be able to honestly fill. When you feel drained, would be enough to fill with positive energy, feeding on rare pieces of art and sipping drops of rock music, hoping that this lady Life can surprise us in all its forms and in all its wonderful colors. Observe all colors of mankind should make us happy, honored and gratified. There is nothing better to appreciate in a healthy and relaxed all

those colors that the world has given us with its
multicolored breeds populations.

CHAPTER THREE
Google, Twitter, Facebook and Youtube between the notes of the time and dreams

Some people asked about the future and not finding adequate responses mingles between pages ideals of Google, Twitter, Facebook &

Youtube in order to realize those desires that no one would have dreamed of following. There are those who hope to create blogs, videos and pages that could have happened between boaters loyal and to make it in the web. Some claim that it is not nice to rest on their laurels, but should not give in to defeat. Some think that the faces shrouded in mystery are the most intriguing of those who wrap themselves in the banality of their appearance. There are those who show her pretty face to get to heaven and who does not show his face to avoid being involved or upset. There are the young newlyweds who flaunt their holiday in style. There are others who put on pedestals their children who would rather be free. Instead, there are those who think that children are creatures to love and care for and never having to show or to use as the finest items: the children, for the simple fact of being such, they have the clear right to live in serene land where you can always smile and be followed in the most exemplary for all. Some think that the wise and serious expression of a child can put more embarrassment than any other face. Some believe strongly that everything is exciting and should not be shown in a sentimental invasive and dramatically pathetic in various social, but should be kept tight and intimate between the walls of their home. "The feelings, if they are real and concrete, should not be exposed or bandied about on Google, Twitter, Facebook or Youtube and should not be thrown in people's faces who truly loves. If you hold really a person, you should not externalize on these social networks or in other temporary pages. You should not feel the need to do so. does not make sense. All this would be pointless, tedious or darn intrusive, if you live a sincere feeling of love or friendship. Who can do these stupid outputs is considered pathetic and empty. But it is no wonder if there is some people that is stripped of his most intimate emotions, that you go to see the toilet or another: we live in a society empty, vile and mindless and in a beautiful country of shit named Italy. There's really no wonder. And not to mention the children who are tossed on the first page as if they were refined objects or puppets: they really should be creatures to love, to care for and preserve and not to degrade and exploit. Besides, everything is within the normal process of things that exist in a society that is adrift, like ours, now more than ever. I am not as Google, Twitter, Facebook and Youtube to be shameful, but the use made of it. And then from this story I am getting their losers: the children. They are called into question without their consent and to the delight of adults morons who have this desire to be inhumane always at the forefront and get a lot of "likes". You return home and connect on Google, Twitter, Facebook and Youtube to relax and enjoy themselves after a hard and stressful day and what to see or view !? images and phrases unnecessary and shameful. This is the reality of social networks and the society we live in, unfortunately. " There are those who would not want to grow anything, who often puts into practice the young child who has within himself and those who say "grow up sooner or later", postponing the adult phase of their existence. There are those who consider an eternal boy, enrolling in pages dedicated to the imagination that accompanies us throughout our days without apathy. Instead, there are those who think that the imagination has the same limits of reality, imagining only what you know without ideals. Some like the events and news that are not pathetic, whether stravivere yet another youth and who know how to excite most of the past. They could not miss the cheerful and optimistic people who would never change their lives with no other, who have lived moments of glory and are ready to live another. Instead people more realistic claim that our delicate honesty, our conscience, our soul pure and fresh, although not make us immune from the evils and injustices of others and difficult system of our country, somehow manage to make us proud to exist in the most contented and healthy as possible in this world full of uncertainties and dangers. "One day you think, all in all, the life you've created some very strong emotions difficult to explain and to externalize and will do so only if you trust yourself to the hilt. One day you think it's all over, but there's always that glimmer of hope that gives you the strength to get up and get on with more enthusiasm than before. One day you're there, the next day you're completely absent. There are days and moons. " There's also those Tag it in faded photos from the time classmates, friends of the summer holidays and business associates to find a bit 'of refreshment. Some believe that children be themselves makes us fathers of large and inviting ideas, then there are those who seeks out and met some very special people who could eventually disrupt or involve the life of every day, and who can deal with friends not seen for some time or acquaintances who are light years away. Instead, there are those who think that the distance and remoteness are ready to betray, but lack the ability and the strength to not let us share the different ideas, the many emotions, strange sensations, sweet thoughts and fantastic dreams. There also those who believe strongly that the 20 years they lived intensely a lot 'of time ago, but they are within us with kind soul and he does not want to go to fortune, and you try to pick them up and catch them with enthusiasm a little warm but pleasant, taking advantage of their generosity. Since time flies not coming back, trying very firmly grasp the present moment. There is the handsome actor, dancer elegant, clever comedian, writer emerging, trying to get noticed in all their performances to be there, to survive, to transmit all that others would never have allowed you to do. There is a nostalgic vain who thinks strongly that the years fly without mercy, without giving us a chance to stop them, the years fly and we are flying with them with great enthusiasm, with joy to play with it, by force of capture them and to live them intensely as ever. There is a nostalgic discreet argues that healthy rivers of nostalgia and sincere of a past lived intensely flood our mind, but life is now. There are those who find an old friend, but not a new treasure and those who think they have met the true love, but it was not what he wanted. Some people look back with nostalgia and those watching the future with joy. There are those who like a healthy precursor of tomorrow and those who like a simple homesick. There are those who embrace the time and who escapes. There are those who feel the passing years and who caresses them with good humor. Some are and who would want to be. There is the confident and curious boy who would not want to be a psychic or a magician because the curiosity that lives and reigns in his life essence is disarming to the point that it does not fear the future, even this great interest that exists within him is always ready to welcome him, to hug and to taste it with both hands, as it has done for its great past. Some believe that poetry can be defined only questionable if his verses have not the strength to talk or not to move you absolutely nothing. Some people can remember all your Facebook friends on the day of days writing some thoughts like this: "The day of our birthday is considered happy and sad at the same time. Cheerful why brings us back to the event of the birth and is 'always nice to celebrate that year in more' that gives us a particular emotion. A little 'disconsolate' cause you have to deal with the time you get out of hand, after having squeezed. Anyway that year in more 'that adds to our delightful existence, manages to make less noise and remain soft and smooth, not least thanks to the warmth that is given to us by the people so dear to us. Without that heat our life would be meaningless. "Time will overwhelms with its hopes and its illusions, does not stop even if you beg, flies and you spring without apologizing, he loves us in his own way always asking for something in return, is smart and honest at the same time, we sentence to old age and save us from the banality of the youth that there has never betrayed, leaves us poised in front of different choices without giving a little help to find the right solution, it allows us to remember the wonders and failures of our past, is revealed for what it is when it suits them, he loves us and hates the right thing for him, he always wins. " There also those who believe that giving affection to others give us more strength: it is simply a fact very nice and great value of our life to be pursued at every opportunity. Lucia believes that a tear of nostalgia is nothing more than a gentle drop of joy or sorrow that caresses the soul through the streets and trails of our face. Matthew says that it would be no use crying over spilled milk, because it would be even expired for some time now: by tasting a few sips could present indigestible and not pleasing to our dear health. There is the young schoolboy who plunges in the pages of his favorite music, compared with all that is vital and healthy. There is the old reciprocating poems of love and longing with others in order to feel alive and present. Some write poetic notes, words of love, all kinds of aphorisms, interesting stories to tell: "Each of us has a story to tell or to show off, whatever age you can wear. Each of us has a life of his attractive, exciting, thrilling, exciting, but still personal and only so much to be proud of. Each of us is special in its noble or praiseworthy enterprises but also in delicious and small gestures.

" There are also those who think often the moments of glory and the best years of their lives with great nostalgia: those times will always remain in our memories or historical images are captured in photos as delicious pieces of life. Some even claim that it is not always possible to ask us to respect older people, if they have no care or respect for the young man who needs support and to enjoy the best nectars of Art and Life. Sometimes the cynicism and envy of the elderly wrongdoing unfortunately his intention to be there and prove wise and reassuring. There Fabio who believes strongly that boredom kills, those who know the avoids, managing to save in the most rewarding as possible by deleting it, and those who have not yet tasted able to have some chance to avoid being contaminated. Some people think that to engage in any activity or to realize a dream, at the base of all there should be a different dynamic creativity and ability accompanied by large doses of luck, but this lady Fortune where it was possible to hide to avoid being found often! ? There Manuel who believes that having burnt some stages of its existence has served to grow, to live and to act better, to enjoy their own successes and many errors, to face several obstacles in the most just and rewarding and above for not burning. There Daniela who is convinced that esteem means to love, but love also means to enrich themselves mentally and spiritually appreciating at the same time soul and heart. There Fabrizio who does deal with some difficult subjects, hot, raw and sometimes shocking. There are those who follow him in all battles and themes which is pursuing with vigor and determination. However, those who prefer to talk about sports, entertainment or anything particularly inviting. There are those based groups and create pages to deal with some cases of unsolved murders as the crime of Perugia. And just about this case that tempers begin to heat up and go on the boil: some consider a ruthless killer Amanda and Raffaele, his devoted servant and follower in the murder more raw and stripped of Perugia. "The book by Amanda has had positive worldwide, Raffaele faces a sentence that will mark him for life. The same subject is interviewed on the first RAI network as if it were an angel innocent and frightened. " Sandra is that you ask where you can note the guilt of these strange people, when in the meantime the poor innocents are devoured by their strict conscience for many other reasons that afflict their lives. Tonino is wondering whether it can be also published another book on the experience of it, the devoted servant of the American airhead. There also those who consider them innocent unrelated to this horrendous crime, defending them of all charges against them. The sure thing is real and that the only victim in this whole damn story is the poor English girl who had a great desire to live and realize his precious dreams and projects. According to most users of the poor Meredith is gone also to blame. So innocent and guilty are between groups of FB to say and spread their opinion about one of the most controversial murder cases in the history of Italian crime. And then, on other pages, there is Paola who speaks ill of his former fellow villagers, venting on Facebook and saying something unpleasant to them: he always thought that ignorance and envy have the frigates. yes, just like that, he always thought that he made false and hypocritical. The fact that they accepted and revalued after years of serenity and peace was not a good choice, indeed, appeared as a challenge, although at times engaging and pleasant. How could you possibly think that these ladies present themselves different from how they had left many years before !? Some people never change, no! do not change! nor at a distance of time, neither of space. By doing so they just seem devastated and defeats are no more than those, persons defeats. And Paola always smiles at these strange meanness, yes, smiles, why should not he !? But he learned something from all this: that ignorance and envy devour all those who exercise it, as often happens, and she smiles and flies higher and higher because obviously that is, yes, that's right, that is. Healthy people, real and concrete always apply. His goal was always to see them die of envy and think I succeeded. All in all it can be considered positive the proximity of these people on the Internet: Paola found it intriguing, though not entirely healthy. Yet some of them are of exceptional women and Paola found some silver lining in so many people that he considered stupid and bigoted. She points out that loves everyone, everyone, and this is the life force. There Michael often complains of various virus ravaging his PC and his friend web. Lately there are people who send in his place. He has tried to delete these writings, but supposed to have been already read by recipients. He asks immensely sorry for the victims, but he wrote them. The truth is that there is someone who has made some jokes carnival unwelcome, sending many messages not pleasant for anyone. He noticed it late and would like to recover, apologizing to everyone. He claims not to be able to do things like that, sending private messages so stupid. It had to change passwords because someone did not pleasant jokes (these are people he knows well, who also spoke of events very private). He found that they were his cousins who know by heart his account. Michael thinks that these individuals are wanted revenge on him for something that could relate to his mysterious past. But this story is not the only message to him worry: there are other jokes in bad taste or similar things that are affecting many facebook profiles, such as the pornographic movies that wander sometimes in his diary or someone else. It 'also came to know that there are some strange people who even manage to clone profiles FB, and not to mention other strange viral phenomena that occur frequently on various social networks. Then there is Mark who argues that to grasp the taste and smell of life allows us to find the right way to clean paths and exterminated. Maria says that the clarity of one's soul can get dirty for faults due to increasingly disrespectful of other people. There is also Daniel who wants to share his joy, posting a YouTube video he made. It is simply a short film very nice, thoughtful and attentive to the various problems of today's twenty somethings. It 'a very interesting video, because it reflects the dramatic situation of our country and highlights some of the new generations lived: detailed description of the youth and some split our society, music and words that express the profound and sublime talent of Daniel. There are phrases that affect more than other "Castle ruins and Benefits", "The most difficult activities depend on our will,"

"Consume our time." Our old friend Gabriella believes that beauty can not always be synonymous with youth, but also with our thrill and an interior richness. Laura says that it is better to be envied than pitied, because even envy has its positive part that often results in admiration and hatred, and compassion is also a symptom of denigration. Lydia thinks that laughter caused by stupid jokes abound in the mouths of fools, saying that among the programs Italian, roam the worst comedy of all time. "These people are completely banal and out of place, particularly exalted and offensive toward the helpless. They do absolutely laugh and are also invited in transmissions of prestige. You may wonder why their films are blockbusters. Most likely it was a word of mouth by those who are content to smile for a few jokes unhappy and dramatically discounted. While Totò and Roberto Benigni can be considered the best comedy of the story, these people can be treated like the worst crabs of all time. These individuals were never in the ropes of those bright and awake, that are dramatically trivial. With this we want to emphasize that you can not fall so low uttering idiotic jokes and pointing his finger on some defenseless people. You can question everything: politicians, judges, celebrities, any kind of job, but the kids do not! that you can not let anyone !! And meanwhile, they are followed by many fans. And even call them fans or supporters, would not change anything in the situation uncivilized and ignorance in which you find yourself. Besides, what could be expected from people who live in a beautiful country of shit named Italy, where we want to minimize the obscene situation where lives and rests tragically, giving money and positive consensus at the first clown on duty and without any merit . You can save someone among them? of course!! One of the few artists who can be considered attractive and ingenious is the adorable and amazing Virginia Raffaele. She: Simply delicious and addictive. You could do other clever and original names of comedians like Crozza, Brignano, Marchesini, brothers Guzzanti etc. ". One can not forget that Lucia, FB, is delighted to make philosophical discourses that attract minds thinking. There is also Simona speaking of his favorite authors, Pablo Neruda considering the absolute best, because he writes poems and traces of life simply sublime, really deep and engaging. There Tiziana adoring thoughts which accord with his philosophy of life. Everything about the positivity and personal growth is capturing his attention in the book he is reading: Waine Dyer, Paulo Coelho, Osho, Brian Weiss. It is associated with these comments that Sarah, who often prefer to read books and stories that convey joy and serenity: Paulo Coelho, Sergio Bambaren, Stephen Littleword, Pablo Neruda, can be considered the clear examples of positive and well-being. And Finally, there is our dear Francis wants to share his experience with his own publishing house, claiming that life is always waiting with open arms, is very valuable and to enjoy to the full, trying to accept it and respect it in the most rewarding as possible, also because it could hide its best pearls. Francis wants to share just a few drops of Happiness with dear friends known on Google, Twitter, Facebook and Youtube, expressing its moments of joy and stating that return to be calm and bright as ever, after several trips in the ego due to the magical and complicated experience editorial, is considered a good feeling in a sea of splendor and awe. Tasting these delicious fruits and enjoy these healthy and strong emotions, after deep and delicate excursions in his precious soul and in its severe conscience has no price. In these strenuous journeys of the mind, along the routes of writing and publishing, everything happened, all right: he gave himself to his concerns, he rejoiced and suffered unusually slowly, loved and hated the loneliness, has devoured sorrows and resentment, envy proved he always ignored, knew the evil dark, lost track of time and space, he cried softly, he laughed bitterly, thought trains passed and never caught on the fly, joked with fire arguing with the storms of water, endured the life experiences of others, has absorbed the various feelings of guilt or something, he chewed virtual sand and spat poison and blood, sweat shirts in 1000, wore tank tops or 1000 t-shirts and questioned even the pants she wore to put into practice his ideas 1000, has come to terms with the spirit and with the perception, he saw his face in old age he so unknown, met maturity more intrusive, he even saw the void in an empty room, he experienced the emptiness of a love emptied by vacuum, he felt the void of nothingness, was full of huge voids that were not able to be filled if not with his great soul that was not empty, received total chaos inside and outside him, devoured pieces of boredom and melancholy, insomnia and torment he lived, he tried the vacuum and absence without finding its delicious essence, was intoxicated Internet and has been feeding the worst crap that roamed on Google, Twitter, Facebook and Youtube, has found between virtual people the worst crabs on the earth, saw the darkness and the darkness even when the sun was out, he thought his dear roots and the cursed land, looked at people who had always snubbed and those wretched chatter that has always ignored, saw failures instead of his achievements, he found people who did not think in years, found the anxieties, anxieties and fears, has compared his defeats with victories of others forgetting the great joys lived, he thought about things and facts that he wanted to avoid like the altar and the little children, used maniacally tools that hated as PC and internet, knowing in some compensation as Google, Twitter, Facebook and Youtube, saw himself in other people, refused the intense changes, tried his sweet moans, breathed joy and pain through the streets of his soul. Francis wants to keep in mind that these internal conflicts have been tested and received mostly during the publication of the first seven books, whereas the start of his career has been signed by some experiment or project, in order to enter the delicately into gear writing and publishing. Obviously, to get to the 13 current works, the route was more peaceful and healthy, making happy Soul and Heart. Here's what the danger of writing and what it regards!?. You can live anxieties and fears as if our lives were a living hell, though it seems all a wonder. Get carried away by the magic of writing could be dangerous and you should handle it very carefully. It becomes part of a world in itself, it closed and unique, difficult to study and digest, but easy to love. You may lose control if you are unable to reconcile the inspiration with reality or are unable to handle events editorials from the start. Moreover, for a person like him, it is used in the open air, between one area and one of the most beautiful city in the world, being prepared for dynamic activities and outside the lines, in professions open and addressed to the public, find themselves in a classroom and the other court, including a secretariat and another, between one class and another of a school, between a TV program and another, between one set and the other, could not otherwise happen. We should also point out that publish 13 works, in a short time, it is not to be considered a real walk, but a trip editorial enveloping and engaging, if rather unnerving. In any case, it can be assumed that it was well worth the effort and that other rifarebbe 1000 times an experience so intense and extraordinary. For those who wish to undertake this type of activity so fascinating, it only remains to wish good luck and tenacity, after knowing what might be encountered. But now Francis breathes the serenity found. Now breathe poetic stories and new spells. Now an air of celebration and youth. Now breathe the positive that is in him. Now back to life. And call it pure 5th Rebirth, would not change anything in his long and attractive path of pure freedom. would not change a thing. Also our dear author Francis prefer to use Google, Twitter, Facebook and Youtube to promote her jewelry editorials, having been distributed in every country in the world. Consider the social network of excellent tools to make themselves known to discerning readers, founding groups of great interest, creating pages related to the importance and brilliance of his lyrics and appreciating everything that can appear useful to the advertising thereof. He wants to prove to all his great qualities, his hidden potential, his creative abilities and his mood artistic. Care precious manuals like little children to care for and love and try to protect them in the best way, making his work his reason for living. Again Francis speaks of himself by claiming to be a simple boy and live in simple things chasing the smile of his soul. I do not think that we should thank for kissing the sun and the best star gazing in the archive of his conscience. And 'he who feels grateful to others and himself to beat their hands to all those emotions that have donated to follow him, in reading it and understand it in all its paths of pure and profound freedom. Among the photos linked to his childhood published on Facebook, it is out strangely picture of his childhood, which, according to him, is not one of the best. This face shy, tender and innocent simply want to represent his state of mind, yet another revival, another personal success that is taking place in that period and magical at the same time delicate in his books there is something delicious that child, there is his innocence, his tenacity, his goodness, his love of life, there is its very essence, is first of all his soul, which for him is the place to start and above all, the precise point to return to, because the depth of the soul rest all the photos and experiences of a youth lived with both hands. This is what we wanted, tried or built !? These are the realities and dynamics that are around our beloved social network!?. Some smiles to life by finding solutions anywhere, those who continue to dream in the world of his emotions, who despairs in the chaos of his troubles, who become a young grandmother, who tries to become one of the most prolific publishing world and those who continue to chat in losing anything of his own ignorance. You can not allow those wretched chatter and those stupid silences destroy our spirits and our dignity. You should try to be superior. In order to defeat the ignorance, deceit and hypocrisy, we just have to live like the angels and dolphins, flying happy on the notes of the Soul. Some people think that the best dream is to continue doing everything we like to do without any scruples, continue to raise the bar, to innovate, to have new dreams and have the opportunity to build and advance new and essential projects . There is also the boy lively, not chasing a life without vices, he claims to have done what he liked to do, but the real problem is that often what appeals to him is absolutely not approved the mass.

FOURTH CHAPTER

Social networks between
the popular poetry, art and music.

There is also that girl from that lofty features, on

Google, Twitter, Facebook & Youtube, listen to his favorite music, and closing your delicate eyes do not get nothing but a magical sound and sweet. It plunges in those sublime notes to try the serenity that had vanished among the various daily difficulties. You lose the spell of the sounds found after much soul searching. Finally able to embrace the true strength of his soul to forget the superfluous that surrounds and wins, wins on the boredom and sadness invasive felt decidedly ominous. This is the power that can own only the Goddess of Music, the power to embrace the serenity 'lost. That sweet and delicate sound is nothing but the magic of singing dolphins.

Also on Social they could not miss the true fans and music lovers who, after their own myths and idols, they managed to establish the groups dedicated to living legends like Mina, Renato Zero and Vasco Rossi. Some people wanted to commemorate the 70th anniversary of founding Mina some group like this: Life-Mina, the most beautiful voice of Italy that is good for our health, try it. For those who worship the Lady of Italian Music for excellence, Mar. 25, 2010 celebrated its first 70 years of a wonderful life, after having given more than 50 complete years of successful career. Tiger Cremona Strikes and will continue to do so. Believe it! For those who think that vitamin M is an excellent medicine super natural to solve various moments of despair and boredom intrusive. It 's definitely better than vitamin C !? It 'just the number one. Career and life, were those extraordinary Mina: his songs have undoubtedly made the history of our Italian Music. More than 100 albums recorded and more than 150 million records sold in more than 50 years of wonderful career. It is always present among us and never forgotten with his popularity intact, although it disappeared from the scene. Artist from the thousand-quality interpretive and expressive, is the largest Lady of Italian melodic song. Symbol of times already lived and never forget and undisputed interpreter and protagonist of social and musical stories that never end. This is the Mina yesterday and thankfully even today, the queen of Italian Music.

There are those who devotes a few pages with great verve to his favorite artist Renato Zero, writing some article on the occasion of his 60 years of life:

NINE PRECIOUS JEWELS FOR 60 YEARS OF RENATO:

What better place could be chosen by Renato Zero to celebrate its 60th anniversary in music if not the picturesque scenery of Piazza di Siena, one of the most romantic places in Villa Borghese, in the heart of Rome. "The Event of 2010" would be the name most appropriate to describe the nine shows performed very successfully by the Roman in the enchanting atmosphere of Villa Borghese from September 29 to October 9 of that year. Again the histrionic Renato was brilliant in revisiting the old and the recent successes of his long career in an exemplary manner, failing to meet the expectations of the fans present at the various concerts. Then one could speak of nine delicious unique jewelry and different from each other, with surprises really interesting, thanks to the welcome presence of distinguished guests who came along and displayed on the fantastic stage. The cute Giorgio Panariello, the charming Monica Guerritore, the exciting Carla Fracci, the talented Fiorella Mannoia, the wonderful Raffaella Carrà, the dark Mario Biondi, the great Raf, the Strepitosa Rita Pavone are just some of the Great Artists have ventured to interpret with great professionalism and enthusiasm the famous pieces of expensive Renatone. The nine concerts were the result of great discipline and sacrifice not only by the Roman artist and guests present, but also by all the artistic staff who worked with great commitment and devotion. Dancers very talented to cuddly children who are provided to serve as the beautiful setting on some tracks of Renato. An event unique. Now we just have to wait with the next big fervento masterpieces of one of our favorite poets. Some people often share links and posts dedicated to Pink Floyd rather than those on the Beatles or the Rolling Stones. Pink Floyd, one of the legends of the most noble and prestigious around the world Rock, one of the bands most brilliant in the history of all time. "The Dark Side of the Moon", one of their most famous albums and sold in rock history, celebrates its first 40 years of life, a page of history, an icon immortal. The disc full of class and fantasy is considered the most creative and meaningful in their impeccable career and is also a journey of progressive pop entirely harmonious and evocative. And then there are those who joins the group Nirvana, Led Zeppelin or the one for Guns N'Roses. Instead, there is one who shares more often than the post of the legendary Queen who represented a real institution of the Rock. The Queen, one of the rock formations of the most successful of these last 40 years. Mainly thanks to their sound processed and pompous, the sublime harmony vocals of Freddie Mercury, a musical mixture between glam and hard were always blockbusters. Songs like "We are the champions", "Bohemian Rhapsody", "We Will Rock You", "A kind of magic", "I want to break free", "Radio ga ga", "The show must go on", They signed and topped the soundtrack of our evenings in the company, of our parties in sincere harmony, our dances, our love and disaffection, of our friendships, of our nectars life. And the music of the rock hard and effectively extended, the dark tones in the higher ones, unsurpassed voice the eccentric, excessive and legendary Freddie Mercury. He liked to do things his own way and have fun. If the next day was over all her money would continue to do everything like he had a lot of money, because that's how he used to do, he would go always with a Persian caliph and no one would stop him. He loved to live a full life, and no one could say what he had to do, yes, him, the one who liked to be defining the true queen of the Rock. Speaking of rock, the company can meet the followers of

Vasco, Pelù or Ligabue. Some people create pages devoted to the various performances of Vasco, even putting into question some of his great qualities. There are those who worship him and who implores him, and there are those who are surprised by who mocks him. And then there are those who do not believe the withdrawal of Vasco from great Italian stages or from the extensive music scene. His stage is not 'the altar of his being, his real reason for living, where he managed to find his way to purify and recharge, which can share experiences of love, suffering and hardships of all kinds of any kind, he can convey the true and strong emotions that we can only perceive and care, where he manages to keep his head perched in the clouds and feet firmly on the ground. where you can breathe and savor his musical verve, where it shows a real raging torrent, where everything is pure adrenaline and nothing more than that, which is best read the soul of his rock more and more lively, where everything is granted, even his eternal madness, where everything is amazing respecting one's mind, where everything meets and clashes, real and surreal, magic and poetry, where you can finally show off his true nature adventurous, excessive and evasive, unbridled and unrestrained, succeeding in fabulous intent to please and enrich everyone, absolutely everyone, where he is all-encompassing, yes, him, the one who has marked our parties, our love and disaffection, our nights, our true and dear friendships, our small and big moments of freedom and happiness, our dear Vasco Rossi. Some people simply prefer the Beatles to the Rolling Stones, making everyone know friends through their Facebook page. There also those who remember them with images momentous groups and entire pages. On October 5, the 62 'they released their very first 45 rpm "Love me do" and in the spring of the following year came out' their long-awaited LP "Please Please Me". From then on we saw them fly high. In fact the Beatles jumped topped the charts and established themselves not only for their music simple and overwhelming, but also for the way they wear certain clothes and wear their hair, imposing somehow their way of being young. From that moment onwards azzeccarono songs just to break through social and musical universe. Soon they became the most 'big event of the youth music of all time. So 'it came on the Beatlemania, which were infected millions and millions of individuals, to the present day. There is a diligent collector who shares links of rare works of art and historical pieces of rock music. Instead, there is the guy who wants casual and loose remember the legendary Marilyn Monroe, 50 years after his tragic and mysterious disappearance. Marilyn, sexy symbol of the 50s', fabulous sign of seduction and set of vulnerabilities. "The biggest Diva movie ever existed, with a desire to survive and emerge, proved more radiant and also the extraordinary openness and the wide availability made it the simple girl next door (the anti-diva par excellence) . Eternal enchantress with her provocative optimism continues to hold on us, 50 years after his death proving much more than a sex symbol.

FIFTH CHAPTER

Social networks between
the notes of happiness and freedom

Some people think you find on Google, Twitter, Facebook & Youtube, those smiles that had been stolen from his loved ones enemies and those seeking to taste morsels of happiness that were lost along the way. There are those who are mentally enriched thanks to the values and achievements of others; the matter can not be rewarding if there is no substance: fortunately meet special people who teach us the best nectar of life, and we feed their tempting words, expressions, ideas and opinions, their every thought turns out to be better than a pasta dish, a steak or a delicious dessert.

♪ ♫ The stupidity of some people will stop worrying about if we decide to meet again with our inviting smile. While the first will not bring 'never to great things, the smile will fly to new and attractive achievements. ♪ ♫ smile soothes and makes my heart happy, enriching the mind of those who receive it and who gives. ♪ ♫ The best comedian is not the one who manages to snatch an easy smile, but the person who will have the ability to make us cry with joy. Some argue, in the pages of Google, Twitter, Facebook & Youtube that the moments of happiness' are indefinable and last truly a moment; The real and profound happiness achieved with moderate humility will definitely be better and would be enough to look deep into the heart of our soul.

There are people who are content with mere crumbs to really feel happy and do not claim anything but a warm hug from loved ones and are quite noticeable for their bright humility. There are others who would like to win everything 'that the world can not' offer, even the impossible, to feel more 'strong and powerful, appearing hungry for power dirty and infamous, and have absolutely to follow and praise. There are times when it takes little to be happy and there are other situations in which the extraordinary events make you really sad. Some people, on Google, Twitter, Facebook & Youtube, trying to enjoy those moments of freedom he had lost in a matter of hours of stress and boredom. Some people can find thoughts and words that deal with Lady Liberty. There are others who still believe in the great value of liberty in all its forms: all humanity needs to believe again. Still others think that fail to establish groups and entire pages in praise of freedom as an absolute value. Some people try disgust towards the disciplines imposed by others, only for their taste of power. Some people believe that man is born free rejecting the hypocrisy and the blackmail of those who govern. Some people can find true freedom and experiencing themselves shamelessly showing strengths, weaknesses and character, and then you realize that the freedom we were looking for was just around the corner or in the drawer of our soul always ready to help us kind and gentle.

SIXTH CHAPTER

The 1000 notes of nature and of the heart

There is also the kind attached to their roots trying to find on Facebook or Youtube on the stunning images of the Earth and its plunges in thought devoted to his country, bringing forward some ideas that somehow manage to satisfy his sincere and healthy nostalgia for origins. Some people outside in this way his great love for the homeland. There are those who think that the roots do not love each other the same way and you feel normal periods of boredom and distance that basically are cheered by the fact that the place where you were born you are fortunately in a major angoletto of his own heart. There are those who conceives love with exaltation inner dowry authentic greatness that we manifest in everyday life with expressions of affection. Some consider love as a wonderful adventure in which we set off without thinking, in search of conquests more and more 'intriguing. Some people try to revive the seasons of love or who simply finds the love in every season of the soul. Each season gives us the colors most 'different, sometimes faint, sometimes heated, but still noble and sublime to the point of being considered useful to our mood is not always kind. The variegated colors that always have their appeal and their personal beauty. They are attractive to those who observe them and scrutinizes them with love and wonder. They appear essential and true to the purest souls and thinking. In any case it is the force of nature that deserves his best applause. Some people manage to simply externalize his boundless love for the summer. It was last summer to delight me of his pleasant life essence. It was the summer to save me from the sadness of a winter to forget. Welcome Summer. we will surely agree the two of us, the two of us we understand the fly with you because no one is alone. This year again you'll feed your best nectars, those of a freedom that only you can give me with your warm welcome, that salutary hospitality that only we know adventurers sniff. Some people remember their love for the most beautiful city in the world dedicating some poetry: "Roma, you come, you're lost. Although a bit 'fierce, does not leave any wounded. How many things I wanted to ask you how many fairy tales and I wanted to tell you !? Rome, are a story that never dies, and this you know. A mother very dear and so beautiful, there is your sister. Are you happy to hear me? sometimes I would like to break away, at critical moments and stressful. But strangely I troublest and envelop me with your health pomps. Can you create an interesting and promising, are in my heart always. I'm happy to see you and the way viverti grabbing your best background. You're tough and nerve-wracking, but gifts such strength and tenacity so effectively. I will walk 'on your big streets a bit' bloody, but still unique and perfect. I am famous my poses in front of your beauty always festive. They are always happy, 'cause you exist and persist in my thoughts as yesterday. There are many reasons to adore and I would undress. Hello Mrs. city, help me definitely in trouble. I seek you all the time, I love you immensely with your people that will never betray you. " And then there are those who believe that the best shows we are given by our dear nature with his indomitable will. Mother Earth 'so selfless and genuine that manages to breastfeed plants and trees to life. There also those who believe that the freshness of our souls heated and colored by the return of spring is always excited to gather other opinions, other thoughts, other ideas, other souls with firm humility. There are those who think that the evil cashed in the past you can not forget if you can remember the immense good often received in all these interesting paths of intense life.

The notes and pages of Google, Twitter, Facebook & Youtube colors more 'variety, shapes and content more inviting, open, you browse, read, scrutinize, they love and then close with the hope and the desire to read them again with the same passion that was presented initially

(F.Primerano)

Finito di stampare nel mese di Agosto 2015
per conto di Youcanprint *Self - Publishing*